Job Insecurity isn't Always Efficient

I. Introduction:

Workers value job security. Specifically, they value protection against the possibility that they will lose their job because their skills have become obsolete or have ceased to be a good match for their employer. If at least some workers value job security highly enough, then it is efficient for at least some firms to adopt policies in which they commit, implicitly or explicitly, not to dismiss employees except for "just-cause," in contrast to policies in which employers are free to dismiss employees "at-will." This is true even though just-cause firms have lower average output, which they do because workers remain at their jobs even when their skills become obsolete, and also because some just-cause workers exploit the greater opportunity to shirk afforded by just-cause protection. Just-cause firms can simply offer a correspondingly lower wage, which some workers will accept. There is a tradeoff, and the reduced output can be the (efficient) price paid for increased job security.

The main purpose of this paper is to investigate whether the market efficiently allocates workers to just-cause jobs vs. at-will jobs, and how policy interventions impact total welfare. We show that the unregulated allocation of workers is not generally welfare-maximizing. This is due to the presence of externalities: a non-shirker who joins a just-cause firm raises average output (and hence the wage) for all other just-cause workers, but does not internalize this effect and so is more reluctant to join a just-cause firm than would be efficient. A shirker who joins a just-cause firm has the opposite (also not internalized) effect on wages, and so is inefficiently eager to join a just-cause firm. A policy that encourages just-cause employment will cause some non-shirkers (of whom inefficiently few join just-cause firms) and some shirkers (of whom inefficiently many join just-cause firms) to switch to just-cause firms, and we show that in some circumstances this can be welfare-improving.

2

To see why this is so, consider the effect of a tax on at-will firms, which would have the effect of moving some workers from at-will to just-cause firms. Infra-marginal workers who choose at-will firms even with the tax will be worse off by the amount of the tax (assuming their labor supply elasticity is zero), but this loss will be exactly offset by the government's gain from tax receipts. Infra-marginal workers who choose just-cause firms even without the tax will be affected by it only insofar as it affects the wage that prevails in just-cause firms: an increase in the just-cause wage is necessary and sufficient to make them better off. We show that if workers are paid as part of a class or group, the just-cause wage may increase or decrease as a result of the tax. Marginal workers who switch from at-will to just-cause jobs as a result of the tax will be made strictly worse off if the just-cause wage decreases or stays the same, as these are workers who preferred at-will to just-cause employment absent the tax. This group can only be made better off by a tax if it causes a sufficiently large increase in the just-cause wage. In sum, an increase in the just-cause wage is necessary for the tax to increase total welfare, and a sufficiently large increase in that wage guarantees it.

The ideal policy would be to set the tax (or the subsidy if the market allocation contained too few at-will workers instead of too many[1]) that achieves the welfare-maximizing allocation of workers. If setting the tax at the optimal level is not practically possible, then it becomes worth asking whether a ban on *all* at-will firms (which can be thought of as a sufficiently high tax) can increase welfare even though it will cause there to be inefficiently *many* just-cause firms. We show that a ban can increase or decrease total welfare relative to the unregulated equilibrium.

A key assumption of the model is that in just-cause firms the pay difference between shirkers and non-shirkers must be smaller than the difference in their productivity. If this were not the

---

[1] We focus on potentially welfare-improving taxes on *AW* firms rather than subsidies because it is policies that encourage just-cause protections, not those that discourage them, that are actually proposed.

case (i.e., if workers were paid their marginal products), then the externalities described above would not be present and the unregulated equilibrium would be efficient. Moreover, for just-cause protection to be meaningful, it must limit firms' ability not only to fire workers, but also to cut the wages of workers who the firm would like to be rid of. We assume complete wage compression in just-cause firms.[2]

II. Previous Literature:

It is often argued that employment protections lead to inefficient allocation of resources because firms cannot destroy jobs that have lost their productive value. Furthermore, if job destruction is difficult, it may lead to less job creation and higher unemployment (Lazear (1990), Ljungqvist and Sargent (1998)). But there are also a number of papers that develop models in which employment protection can increase aggregate output. Bertola (2004) shows that requiring risk-neutral firms to insure risk-averse employees against negative income shocks can enhance aggregate output if job switching is costly. The idea is that job switching is likely to be efficient precisely when current income is low, but that is when risk-averse workers are least willing to pay the job-switching costs. Similarly MacLeod & Nakavachara (2007) argue that just-cause employment laws can, under certain conditions, provide workers with better incentives to make relationship-specific investments. In Levine (1991) just-cause employment laws can increase aggregate output by limiting worker shirking.

Even if job protection laws reduce employment or aggregate output, it does not necessarily mean that they are economically inefficient. If workers suffer disutility from job insecurity, then the welfare harm from some reduction in output can be overbalanced by greater security. Pissarides (2001) points out that most models of employment protection ignore this, and hence rule

---

[2] See Section II below for a discussion of the empirical evidence on wage compression.

out the most natural reason why such protections would exist in the first place. He shows that severance payments and advance notice requirements can serve as a form of efficient insurance for risk-averse employees, though the mechanism in his model differs from ours. Blanchard & Tirole (2008) also argue that worker risk-aversion means that layoffs have a social cost that is not internalized by firms, but they argue that forcing firms to pay a layoff tax to internalize this cost is superior to just-cause protection. We do not take a position on the relative effectiveness of alternative government interventions. Instead we focus solely on just-cause protection, which appears to be the relevant policy question in some cases. Moreover, the basic intuition that we develop in this paper may be applicable in other situations where workers and firms bargain over job characteristics, and where the outcome of such bargaining can be sub-optimal. See the discussion in Section V below for such an example.

Like the majority of this literature, our model acknowledges that just-cause protection results in some workers remaining in their firms even when their skills become obsolete or are no longer a good match. Another key element of our model is that some workers are "shirkers" who will shirk if they work in just-cause firms. The only other paper we know of that focuses on the impact of shirking is Levine (1991). In Levine's model, at-will firms must pay efficiency wages to induce effort, which results in equilibrium unemployment. This inefficiency can be mitigated by having workers post performance bonds which they forfeit if they are fired for shirking. But workers will be unwilling to post such bonds with at-will employers for fear that the employers will fire them and appropriate the bond even if they don't shirk. Since just-cause firms, by assumption, credibly commit not to do this, they can make more use of bonds and so need to rely less heavily on efficiency wages (which cause equilibrium unemployment) to induce effort. On the other hand, some workers in just-cause firms will shirk. Levine shows that there are parame-

5

ter values for which total employment, and hence total welfare (in the Levine paper there is no disutility from avoiding job insecurity, so welfare depends only on employment), is higher if all firms are just-cause firms.

Levine then shows that there are parameter values for which total welfare is higher if all firms are just-cause firms, but for which an individual just-cause firm could not survive, as a single just-cause firm will attract a disproportionate number of shirkers. This result depends on the assumption that there is some cost (Levine calls it a "mobility" cost) associated with working for the single just-cause employer that shirkers will be more willing to pay than non-shirkers.

Our paper is similar to Levine's in that there is adverse selection of shirkers into just-cause jobs. But our mechanism is simpler and we think more general. We do not rely upon efficiency wages, performance bonds, or mobility costs. Rather our model is driven by the fact that individual job choice decisions involve externalities for other workers in the job class. Also, our model allows for the possibility of a welfare-improving tax on at-will firms instead of a complete ban. In Section IV below we show an example in which a small tax on at-will firms is welfare-increasing relative to the unregulated equilibrium, but a full ban is not.

Just-cause protection would have little effect if firms could radically cut workers' wages rather than firing them outright. Furthermore, as discussed above significant wage compression is necessary for our model to work. We assume that all workers in just-cause firms earn the same wage. There is a substantial literature on wage compression in firms. Government and union jobs have significant wage compression that may impact wage dispersion in the entire economy (DiNardo, Fortin, & Lemieux (1996)). But wage compression has been empirically documented in other job settings (Baker, Gibbs, & Holmstrom (1994), Frank (1984)). Pay compression may persist because differences in pay for the same job can lead to morale problems, and because workers may accept within-firm status as a reward for hard work even if not paid their full marginal product (Campbell & Kamlani (1997), Frank (1984)).

III. Model Setup:

A. Sectors.

There are two sectors in the economy, similar to those in Bulow & Summers (1986). In "primary" sector firms production is complex, and workers are only productive if their skills are current (and if they don't shirk). Primary sector workers whose skills are current (and who don't shirk) produce output equal to η, while primary sector workers whose skills are obsolete produce zero.[3] In the "secondary" sector production is simple, and all workers produce an output of θ (if they don't shirk).[4] That is, workers in the secondary sector produce less than primary sector workers whose skills are current, but more than primary sector workers whose skills are obsolete.

B. Firms.

There are two types of primary sector firms. "At-will" (*AW*) firms can fire workers for having obsolete skills or for shirking. "Just-Cause" (*JC*) firms commit not to fire workers for having obsolete skills, so working for a *JC* firm represents a form of insurance against having one's skills lose their value. But *JC* firms can only fire workers for shirking if they can prove to a third party that the shirking took place. We assume that shirking can always be detected, but that it is too costly to prove, so shirkers in *JC* firms are not fired. So in equilibrium there are no termina-

---

[3] An equivalent alternative to skills becoming obsolete is for a worker and a firm to cease to be a good match.
[4] We assume that it is not worthwhile for primary sector firms to try to match with old workers. This means that no fired worker will get another job in the primary sector. It also means that no old non-shirker will quit a *JC* firm and join an *AW* firm, even if their skills are not obsolete.

7

tions in either type of firm. In *JC* firms, not even shirkers can be fired, and in *AW* firms, the threat of being fired gives even shirkers the incentive to work hard.

Following Levine (1991), we assume that *JC* firms cannot cut the wages of those workers known to be shirkers: all *JC* workers are paid the same wage.[5] Secondary sector jobs require no skill and are always available, so no secondary-sector worker would have any reason to accept a lower wage in exchange for job security, which means that all secondary sector firms are *AW* firms and no secondary sector workers shirk. All firms employ constant returns to scale production technologies, so firms can be of any size, and all firms operate in perfectly competitive product markets and earn zero profits, so all output is paid out as wages.

C. Workers and Wages.

A "non-shirker" is defined as a worker who will never shirk, and a "shirker" as a worker who will shirk if he or she can get away with it. That is, non-shirkers never shirk regardless of which type of firm they are in, whereas shirkers shirk in *JC* firms but not in *AW* firms.

All workers live for two periods: young and old. Each young worker is endowed with up-to-date skills and joins a primary sector firm. With probability ρ the worker's skills remain current when old, and with probability $(1-\rho)$ they become obsolete. In *JC* firms workers with obsolete skills cannot be fired, and they do not quit as long as utility in the *JC* firm is higher than utility in the secondary sector. In *AW* firms, these workers are fired and forced into the secondary sector. This lack of job security in *AW* firms is a source of disutility, due either to risk-aversion or to the negative psychological effect of being fired. In the numerical examples in this paper, we focus

---

[5] To approximate wage compression, we could model a scenario where shirkers are paid somewhat less than non-shirkers, but not their actual marginal product, and not enough to discourage shirking behavior. For simplicity in exposition, we assume the shirker and non-shirker wages are not only similar, but identical. See Section II for a discussion of the empirical literature on wage compression.

only on the risk-aversion effect. For a worker i, this disutility is represented by α_i which has (for both shirkers and non-shirkers) a probability distribution function $f(\alpha)$ with support $[\alpha^{MIN}, \alpha^{MAX}]$. This distribution is the same for shirkers and for non-shirkers.

A worker in an AW firm earns η with certainty when young. When old, that worker faces a gamble (skills may or may not turn out to be obsolete) with an expected value of $\rho\eta + (1-\rho)\theta$. The risk associated with this gamble is the source of disutility from job insecurity. Let X represent the certainty equivalent, the amount of guaranteed money that would make a worker equally well-off as the gamble, and let α_i be the difference between $\rho\eta + (1-\rho)\theta$ and X. Using a Constant Relative Risk Aversion utility function for wages $U(w) = (w^{1-\sigma}-1)/(1-\sigma)$, a worker i's expected wage utility from the gamble is $U(w) = \rho(\eta^{1-\sigma i}-1)/(1-\sigma_i) + (1-\rho)(\theta^{1-\sigma i}-1)/(1-\sigma_i)$, and the certainty equivalent is $X = ((1-\sigma_i)U(w)+1)^{1/(1-\sigma i)}$. This gives us the following expression for α_i:

$$(1) \qquad \alpha_i = \rho\eta + (1-\rho)\theta - \left(\rho(\eta^{1-\sigma_i}-1) + (1-\rho)(\theta^{1-\sigma_i}-1) + 1\right)^{\frac{1}{1-\sigma_i}}$$

There is a mass of non-shirkers of measure N^{NS} and a mass of shirkers of measure N^{S}. The mass of non-shirkers who join JC firms (N^{NS}_{JC}) is equal to N^{NS} times the fraction of non-shirkers for whom $\alpha_i > \alpha^{NS}$, where α^{NS} is the (endogenous) threshold level of α_i above which a non-shirker prefers a JC firm to an AW firm. Similarly, the mass of shirkers who join JC firms (N^{S}_{JC}) is equal to the total mass of shirkers N^{S} times the fraction of shirkers for whom $\alpha_i > \alpha^{S}$, where α^{S} is defined analogously to α^{NS}.

Since no one (including shirkers) shirks in AW firms, the wage in primary sector AW firms is equal to η, and the wage in secondary sector firms (all of which are AW firms) is equal to θ. We assume that $\eta > \theta > e$, so that output is greater in the primary sector than in secondary sector (if skills are not obsolete), and that exerting effort is always efficient, even in the secondary sector.

Utility is linear and additively separable in expected wages, disutility from exerting effort, and disutility from lacking job security. The lifetime utility U_{AW} of a worker who joins a primary sector AW firm when young (ignoring discounting) is:

(2) $$U_{AW} = \eta + \rho\eta + (1-\rho)\theta - 2e - \alpha_i$$

Let w_{JC} be the wage in JC firms. The lifetime utility U_{JC}^{NS} of a non-shirker who joins a JC firm when young is:

(3) $$U_{JC}^{NS} = 2w_{JC} - 2e$$

The lifetime utility U_{JC}^{S} of a shirker who joins a JC firm when young is:

(4) $$U_{JC}^{S} = 2w_{JC}$$

Note that (3) and (4) only differ by $2e$, which is the disutility cost of effort that is borne by non-shirkers but not by shirkers.

Shirkers in JC firms all shirk and produce zero output, so all output in JC firms is produced by non-shirkers. Half of the non-shirkers are young and produce output of η. The other half are old, and a proportion ρ of them also produce η. The rest of the old non-shirkers produce zero. So the average output of a non-shirker in a JC firm is $(\eta + \rho\eta)/2$. The JC wage w_{JC} is equal to:

(5) $$w_{JC} = \frac{\dfrac{\eta + \rho\eta}{2} N_{JC}^{NS}}{N_{JC}^{NS} + N_{JC}^{S}} = \frac{\dfrac{\eta + \rho\eta}{2} N^{NS} \displaystyle\int_{\alpha^{NS}}^{\alpha^{MAX}} f(\alpha)d\alpha}{N^{NS} \displaystyle\int_{\alpha^{NS}}^{\alpha^{MAX}} f(\alpha)d\alpha + N^{S} \displaystyle\int_{\alpha^{S}}^{\alpha^{MAX}} f(\alpha)d\alpha}$$

Total output in a JC firm is equal to the average non-shirker output times N_{JC}^{NS}, which according to our wage compression assumption is divided equally among all $N_{JC}^{NS} + N_{JC}^{S}$ JC workers.

D. Thresholds.

Recall that the threshold level of the disutility from lacking job security above which non-shirkers prefer *JC* firms to *AW* firms is called α^{NS}, and that the corresponding threshold for shirkers is called α^{S}.

Lemma 1: $\alpha^{S} = \alpha^{NS} - 2e$

Proof: A non-shirker is indifferent between the two sectors if:

(6) $\qquad 2w_{JC} - 2e = \eta + \rho\eta + (1-\rho)\theta - 2e - \alpha^{NS} \Rightarrow \alpha^{NS} = \eta + \rho\eta + (1-\rho)\theta - 2w_{JC}$

A shirker is indifferent between the two sectors if:

(7) $\qquad 2w_{JC} = \eta + \rho\eta + (1-\rho)\theta - 2e - \alpha^{S} \Rightarrow \alpha^{S} = \eta + \rho\eta + (1-\rho)\theta - 2w_{JC} - 2e$

These expressions only implicitly define α^{NS} and α^{S} because w_{JC} depends on the thresholds. Nevertheless, it is immediate that (6) and (7) differ by $2e$. ∎

The α^{NS} threshold level in (6) is the difference in the expected wage for a non-shirker who chooses an at-will firm and one who chooses a just-cause firm. The α^{S} threshold in (7) is the difference in the expected wage minus the effort cost that shirkers only bear if they choose an at-will firm. So the only difference between shirkers and non-shirkers is that shirkers in *JC* firms get $2e$ more utility than do non-shirkers. The fact that $\alpha^{NS} > \alpha^{S}$ means that the fraction of non-shirkers who join *JC* firms must be (weakly) smaller than the fraction of shirkers who do so:[6] working in a *JC* firm is always more attractive to a shirker than it is to an otherwise equivalent non-shirker.

---

[6] This will be true even if the two distributions are not identical, as long as the disutility from job insecurity is not too much greater among shirkers than it is among non-shirkers.

E. Equilibrium.

A combination $\{N_{JC}^{NS}, N_{JC}^{S}, w_{JC}\}$ is an equilibrium if equations (5) – (7) are satisfied. Rearranging terms in equation (6) shows that the number of non-shirkers that will join JC firms at wage w_{JC} is determined by the distribution of α_i. Similarly, the number of shirkers that will join JC firms at wage w_{JC} is determined by the distribution of α_i and Equation (7). Notice that for any w_{JC}, there is a specific combination of non-shirkers and shirkers that will be attracted to join JC firms. This means, for example, that it is not possible for a firm to choose to attract 20 non-shirkers and 0 shirkers.

Depending on the distribution of α_i, there may be mass points at multiple levels, equations (5) – (7) may be satisfied at multiple points $\{N_{JC}^{NS}, N_{JC}^{S}, w_{JC}\}$ and there may be multiple stable equilibria. The general model with an unrestricted α_i suggests that policy changes can have almost any impact. But if we restrict the distribution of α_i to have nice properties (such as continuity, convexity, etc.), we can say more about the equilibrium.

For example, if α_i is distributed continuously and uniformly, equations (6) and (7) define an increasing piece-wise linear relationship between w_{JC} and the number of non-shirkers and of shirkers. Based on the labor availability $N^{NS} > N_{JC}^{NS} > 0, N^{S} > N_{JC}^{S} > 0$, Figure 1 shows the set of attainable labor market combinations $\{N_{JC}^{NS}, N_{JC}^{S}\}$ for any w_{JC}.[7] For ease of exposition, call this set of attainable combinations curve **A**. There are three line segments in curve **A**. At very low wages, as w_{JC} increases the number of shirkers attracted to the firm is increasing, but no non-shirkers would work for a JC firm. Then, as w_{JC} increases into the middle range, a specific posi-

---

[7] The parameters underlying Figures 1 and 2 were chosen to produce clear pictures and have no particular significance.

12

tive combination $N_{JC}^{NS} > 0, N_{JC}^{S} > 0$ is attracted to the firm. Then, once all shirkers are at JC firms, as w_{JC} increases further, only the number of non-shirkers is increasing.

Figure 1

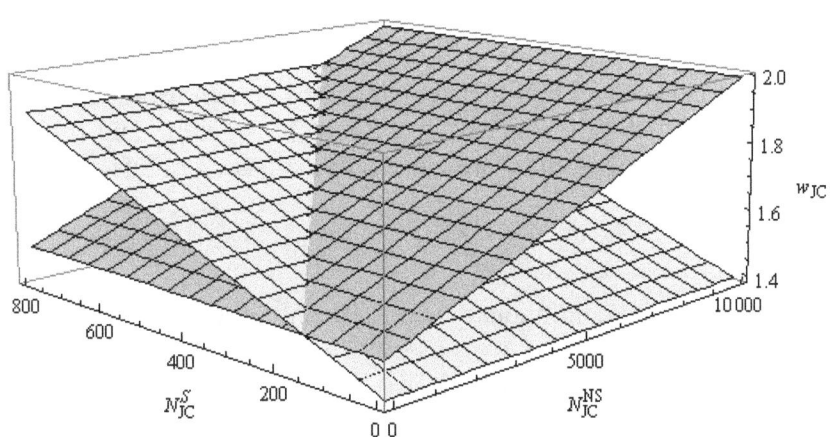

Equation (5) represents the fact that the JC wage must be equal to average output. It can be graphed as a curve in the same three-dimensional space as Figure 1. An equilibrium exists when equation (5) crosses curve **A**, as indicated in Figure 2.

Figure 2

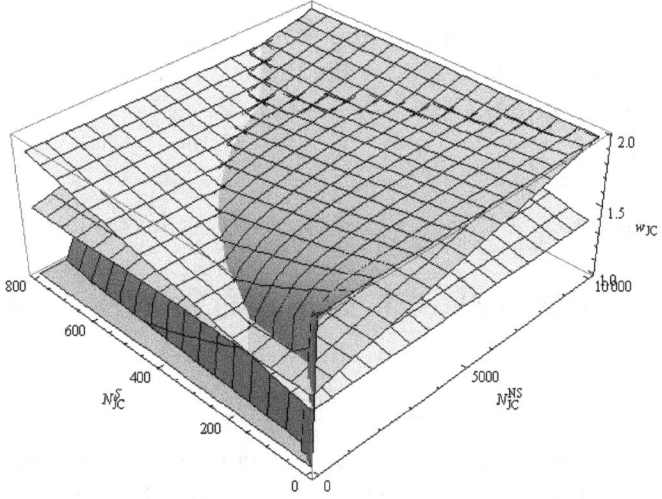

There is always at least one crossing point because Equation (5) crosses curve **A** at the origin, where no just-cause firms operate. Along the first line segment of curve **A**, equation (5) is below curve **A**. In this segment, $N_{JC}^{NS} = 0$ and by equation (5), $w_{JC} = 0$. Starting in the middle segment, when $N_{JC}^{NS} > 0$, it is possible for equation (5) to cross curve **A** from below, and then possibly again from above.

Lemma 2: If α_i is distributed continuously and uniformly, for the attainable labor combinations in the middle segment of curve **A** in Figure 1, equation (5) is increasing and strictly concave. If equation (5) is increasing and strictly concave in the middle segment, and if curve **A** is increasing and linear in the middle segment, there are zero to two crossing points.

Proof: See appendix.

Proposition 1: If α_i is distributed continuously and uniformly, there is at most one stable equilibrium other than $N_{JC}^{NS} = 0, N_{JC}^{S} = 0, w_{JC} = 0$.[8]

Proof: As noted above, equation (5) starts out below curve **A**, so the first crossing point must be from below. But this is not a stable equilibrium. To see why, suppose that a small number of additional workers join *JC* firms, such that they reach a point on the line somewhere above the equilibrium. When the curve crosses the line from below, this causes the *JC* wage to increase to a level above that represented by the line (i.e., above the wage necessary to make those extra workers want to join *JC* firms), which means that other workers would want to follow the first ones and switch to *JC* firms as well, moving even further away from the equilibrium. If equation (5) does not cross curve **A** a second time, this instability will lead to an equilibrium where $N_{JC}^{NS} = N^{NS}, N_{JC}^{S} = N^{S}$.

If equation (5) does cross curve **A** a second time, this time from above, this crossing point will be a stable equilibrium, because moving up the line will generate a wage below that represented by the line, and so below the wage necessary to make those workers want to stay in *JC* firms, which pushes back towards the equilibrium. ∎

We view the equilibrium at $N_{JC}^{NS} = 0, N_{JC}^{S} = 0, w_{JC} = 0$ as less interesting because it tends to have lower welfare than the other stable equilibrium. (If there are no *JC* firms operating, it is eas-

---

[8] This proposition is not fully general. This is because we are ignoring the third line segment where all the shirkers are in the just-cause firms. The slope of equation (5) jumps up when we stop following it along the middle segment and start following it along the third segment. Because of this jump, it is possible to have a third and fourth crossing point. The third crossing point would be from below and would not be stable. The fourth crossing point may be stable, but in that equilibrium all shirkers are in *JC* firms so there is no shirking cost from moving additional workers to *JC* firms. This makes it is trivial to show that a tax or ban can be beneficial. Therefore, we focus on the second crossing point in the middle line segment in the main discussion in this paper.

ier to show that a ban or tax on AW work can be beneficial.) The $N_{JC}^{NS} = N^{NS}, N_{JC}^{S} = N^{S}$ case is also less interesting because there is no impact from a policy towards JC employment. Therefore, in the remainder of the paper, we focus on situations with the intermediate equilibrium characterized as the second crossing point between equation (5) and the middle segment of curve **A**.[9]

IV. Results:

A. Effect on the JC Wage of a Tax on AW Firms.

We consider the effect of a per-worker tax τ on primary-sector AW firms. Equations (6) and (7) show that as the wage differential between AW and JC jobs falls, the thresholds α^{NS} and α^{S} also fall.[10] Lemma 1 shows that α^{NS} and α^{S} must always differ by $2e$, which means that the tax must cause the two thresholds to decrease by the same amount, which we call Δ. The tax will cause some marginal workers to switch from AW to JC firms, which will change the wage in JC firms from w_{JC} to w'_{JC}, which is equal to:

$$
(8) \qquad w'_{JC} = \frac{\dfrac{\eta + \rho\eta}{2} N^{NS} \displaystyle\int_{\alpha^{NS}-\Delta}^{\alpha^{MAX}} f(\alpha)d\alpha}{N^{NS} \displaystyle\int_{\alpha^{NS}-\Delta}^{\alpha^{MAX}} f(\alpha)d\alpha + N^{S} \displaystyle\int_{\alpha^{S}-\Delta}^{\alpha^{MAX}} f(\alpha)d\alpha}
$$

Lemma 3: w'_{JC} can be greater or less than w_{JC}. When α_i is distributed uniformly, $w'_{JC} > w_{JC}$. When α_i is distributed on the U-quadratic distribution, there are parameter values such that $w'_{JC} < w_{JC}$.

Proof: The first statement is immediate from comparing (5) and (8). The second and third statements are proven in the appendix. ∎

---

[9] While we have assumed α_i is distributed uniformly, there are other distributions of α_i such that there will be only one stable equilibrium for reasons similar to those discussed above.

[10] If the tax was also levied on secondary-sector AW firms, the welfare effects would be unchanged, as the loss to the secondary-sector workers would be exactly offset by the gain to the government.

The effect on the *JC* wage of a tax on *AW* firms depends on whether the tax causes the proportion of non-shirkers in *JC* firms to increase or decrease, which in turn is determined by whether the proportion of non-shirkers among those who switch from *AW* to *JC* firms as a result of the tax is larger or smaller than the proportion of non-shirkers among infra-marginal *JC* workers. This can go either way, because in the presence of wage compression, individual job choices have external effects. Each non-shirker who switches to a *JC* firm raises the proportion of non-shirkers among *JC* workers, and so raises the wage for all *JC* workers. Similarly each shirker lowers the *JC* wage, but neither takes this into account when deciding which type of firm to work in. A tax on *AW* firms will cause some non-shirkers to switch and increase the wage, and some shirkers to switch and lower it. The net effect depends on the composition of the group of switchers relative to the composition of infra-marginal *JC* workers, which in turn depends on the distribution of α_i.

B. Total Welfare Effects of a Tax or a Ban on At-Will Firms.

In this section we consider the effect on total social welfare of a tax on *AW* firms, and also of a complete ban on *AW* firms, which we model simply as a tax large enough that no primary sector firms choose to be an *AW* firm. Total welfare adds up the utility for all agents in the economy, including the utility from the work effort that shirkers in *JC* firms are spared. If effort saved through shirking were excluded in the welfare calculation, then a tax or a ban would be less likely to be welfare improving, as then the lost output from moving shirkers into *JC* firms would not be partially offset by the fact that those shirkers were spared the disutility of effort.

Proposition 2: A tax τ on *AW* firms may increase or decrease total welfare, and a ban on *AW* employment may increase or decrease total welfare.

16

Proof: A tax τ reduces the real wage of infra-marginal AW workers by τ. This is a direct transfer from those workers to the government, and so has no effect on total welfare. The effect of the tax on infra-marginal JC workers is:

$$(9) \qquad N^{NS} \int_{\alpha^{NS}}^{\alpha^{MAX}} 2(w'_{JC} - w_{JC}) f(\alpha) d\alpha + N^{S} \int_{\alpha^{S}}^{\alpha^{MAX}} 2(w'_{JC} - w_{JC}) f(\alpha) d\alpha$$

The sign of this effect depends only on the sign of $w'_{JC} - w_{JC}$, which Lemma 3 shows can be positive or negative. The effect on marginal workers is:

$$(10) \; N^{NS} \int_{\alpha^{NS}-\Delta}^{\alpha^{NS}} \left(\alpha + 2w'_{JC} - \left((1+\rho)\eta + (1-\rho)\theta\right) \right) f(\alpha) d\alpha + N^{S} \int_{\alpha^{S}-\Delta}^{\alpha^{S}} \left(\alpha + 2w'_{JC} - \left((1+\rho)\eta + (1-\rho)\theta\right) \right) f(\alpha) d\alpha$$

A worker (shirker or non-shirker) who switches from an AW firm to a JC firm gains the JC wage (for two periods), and also gains α_i because that worker no longer experiences the disutility of job insecurity. That worker loses the expected wage in the AW firm. The net effect is negative if $w'_{JC} \leq w_{JC}$, because these marginal workers preferred to work in AW firms when the JC wage was w_{JC}. So a strictly positive JC wage increase is necessary for this group to be made better off. The net effect of the tax is the sum of (9) and (10). Below we show by numerical examples that this can be positive or negative.

The total welfare effect of a ban on AW employment is:

$$(11) \qquad N^{NS} \int_{\alpha^{MIN}}^{\alpha^{NS}} \left(\alpha - \frac{(1-\rho)\theta}{2} \right) f(\alpha) d\alpha + N^{S} \int_{\alpha^{MIN}}^{\alpha^{S}} \left(\alpha - \left(\frac{\eta}{2} + \frac{\rho\eta + (1-\rho)\theta}{2} \right) \right) f(\alpha) d\alpha$$

In the case of a ban, there are no infra-marginal AW workers, there are only infra-marginal JC workers and switchers. All switchers (both shirkers and non-shirkers) who were in AW firms before the ban gain α_i. The other effects of the ban are simply its effects on total output. For non-shirkers, the ban negatively effects total output because a fraction $(1-\rho)/2$ of them will be old workers with obsolete skills who will remain in a primary sector JC firm and produce zero instead of joining a secondary sector firm and producing θ, as they would have done if they had joined primary sector AW firms when young. For shirkers, there will be a larger loss in output, equal to their total expected output in a primary sector AW firm. Below we show with numerical examples that the expression in (11) can be positive or negative. ∎

Figures 3-5 graphically illustrate how welfare changes in response to changes in the tax on AW firms. The x-axis represents the size of the tax, and the y-axis represents utility. Moving from left to right, as the tax τ on AW employment increases, this lowers the wage in AW firms, causing workers to switch to *JC* firms. At the far right is a tax high enough that it amounts to a ban on *AW* firms. In Figure 3, the parameter values are as follows. The labor productivity variables are set at η=3, and θ=1: secondary sector work is less productive than primary sector work as long as the worker's skills are not obsolete. The probability ρ is set at .98, so most workers' skills do not become obsolete when they are old. The effort cost is set at a fairly low level of e=0.1. And 5% of workers are shirkers, $N^S/(N^S + N^{NS})$=.05. The distribution of σ_i is chosen so that the dis-utility of job insecurity α_i is distributed uniformly on $[\alpha^{MIN}, \alpha^{MAX}] = [0,1.51]$. As described in Section III.C above, α^{MAX} corresponds to the most risk-averse agent ($\sigma_i = 10$), and α^{MIN} corresponds to the least risk-averse agent ($\sigma_i = 0$).

To interpret Figure 3, start at the unregulated equilibrium. Because α_i is distributed uniformly, each incremental increase in τ causes a constant number of workers to switch from *AW* to *JC* firms, a constant proportion of which are non-shirkers. The skills of some of these switching non-shirkers will become obsolete when they are old, but they will nevertheless remain in *JC* firms and produce zero instead of switching to the secondary sector and producing θ, as they would have done had they joined an *AW* firm when young. This is a marginal social cost caused by the tax. Another marginal social cost of the tax comes from the fact that some of the switchers are shirkers. These switching shirkers did not shirk in their old *AW* firms (nobody shirks in *AW* firms), but they do shirk in their new *JC* firms. The sum of these two costs is represented by the dots in Figure 3. This marginal social cost curve jumps discretely down at the level of τ such that all shirkers are in *JC* firms. Once all shirkers are in *JC* firms, the only cost of moving additional workers to *JC* firms is the marginal cost of obsolete skills.

The tax also has a social benefit against which these social costs must be traded off, which is that the workers who switch from *AW* to *JC* firms are spared the disutility of lacking job security.

18

The marginal benefit of an incremental increase in τ (represented by the triangles in Figure 3) is the marginal disutility from job insecurity that the workers no longer experience. This is downward-sloping because the marginal workers that are induced to switch as τ increases have successively lower disutility of job insecurity, and it is linear because α_i is distributed uniformly. The slope of this line changes at the tax rate such that all shirkers are in *JC* firms, because there are fewer total switching workers for a given increase in τ. But because shirkers are only 5% of the marginal workers, and because shirkers' disutility values are near zero near the jump point, the change in slope is very minor. This kink is more noticeable when shirkers make up a greater proportion of the marginal workers.[11]

Total social welfare is represented by the filled squares in Figure 3. Note that this is not on the same scale as the other lines and curves in the figure, as it represents total utility and the others represent components of marginal utility. They are presented together in the same figure to illustrate how the relationships between the marginal social costs and benefits affect total welfare. Starting at the unregulated equilibrium and moving to the right, at first an increase in τ causes total welfare to increase because the workers who move from *AW* firms to *JC* firms as a result have high disutility from job insecurity. But at certain point the marginal benefit of the tax becomes smaller than the marginal cost and total welfare begins to fall. When τ becomes high enough that all shirkers are in *JC* firms, the total marginal cost drops discretely and falls below the marginal benefit, and total welfare discretely increases. But the marginal benefit continues to fall as τ increases, and eventually it once again falls below the total marginal cost and so total welfare starts to fall. For the parameter values represented by Figure 3, a tax on *JC* firms high enough that no *AW* firms exist (which is equivalent to a total ban on *AW* firms) causes welfare to increase rela-

_____

[11] A property of the uniform distribution is that the proportion of shirkers among switchers is the same as their proportion in the population.

tive to the unregulated equilibrium. But a ban is not the first-best policy, because a smaller (but still positive) tax results in welfare that is even higher. A ban "overshoots" the optimum, eliminating all AW firms when the optimal number of such firms is positive.

In Figure 3, the probability that skills become obsolete was set at a low level ($\rho=.98$). Figure 4 displays what happens if the parameter values are the same as in Figure 3 except that the probability a worker's skills become obsolete is higher ($\rho=.94$). This causes the marginal social cost due to skill obsolescence to increase, which pushes the total welfare curve downward. In this case a ban on AW employment makes society worse off relative to the unregulated equilibrium, though the welfare-maximizing level of τ is still positive.

In Figure 5 we return to the parameter values in Figure 3, but we make one change. In Figures 3 and 4 we let σ_i be distributed on $[0,10]$ in such a way that α_i is distributed uniformly on $[\alpha^{MIN}, \alpha^{MAX}]$. In Figure 5 we let σ_i be distributed uniformly on $[0,10]$. Since, as described in Section III.C above, α_i is a non-linear function of σ_i, in this figure the distribution of α_i will not be uniform. There is no specific name for the distribution of α_i in this case, but it is similar to the U-quadratic distribution discussed in the appendix. Specifically, this distribution has more mass in its tails.

There are several differences between Figure 5 and the previous figures. First, because of the mass in the tails, for each unit increase in the tax on AW firms, more workers are moved to JC firms, and so the cost of obsolete skills is increasing. Second, without a uniform distribution of α_i, an increase in the tax does not move over a fixed proportion of shirkers. In this example, for each unit increase in the tax on AW firms, an increasing proportion of shirkers are moved to JC firms, so that the marginal social cost due to shirking is increasing. Third, the marginal social gain is also not linear: for each unit tax increase there is an increasing number of marginal workers but because disutility values are still falling, the net result is a decreasing but non-linear marginal social benefit curve. Overall in Figure 5, a positive tax on *AW* firms attracts more shirkers to the *JC* firms, which makes it difficult for a ban or a tax on *AW* firms to be welfare-improving. Specifically, for the parameter values represented by Figure 5, *any* tax on *AW* firms will lower welfare.

C. Necessary Conditions for a Tax on AW firms to be Welfare-Increasing.

In the above examples, we show that a tax or a ban on *AW* firms can either increase or decrease total welfare. In this sub-section, we show some necessary conditions for a ban to be welfare-increasing.

Corollary to Proposition 2: A necessary condition for a tax to increase total welfare is that $w'_{JC} > w_{JC}$.

Proof: The proof to Proposition 2 showed that: (i) the effect of a tax on infra-marginal *AW* workers is exactly offset by the effect on the government; (ii) the effect on infra-marginal *JC* workers has the same sign as the *JC* wage change; and (iii) the effect on marginal switchers is negative if $w'_{JC} \leq w_{JC}$. Thus $w'_{JC} > w_{JC}$ is a necessary condition for a tax on *AW* employment to be welfare-increasing. ∎

The condition that $w'_{JC} > w_{JC}$ is necessary for a tax on *AW* firms to be welfare-increasing. So an empirically-based prediction that a proposed tax would make the *JC* wage go down would be sufficient to conclude without further analysis that such a policy would reduce welfare. While the $w'_{JC} > w_{JC}$ condition is necessary, it is not sufficient. For example in Figures 3 and 4, the fact that α_i is distributed uniformly means that the *JC* wage always gets higher the higher the tax (see Lemma 3), yet there are still some levels of τ that result lower welfare than in the unregulated equilibrium. We do not have a general sufficient condition for a tax on *AW* firms to be welfare-increasing. But we observe that both infra-marginal *JC* workers and marginal switchers are better off the higher the *JC* wage, and no one is worse off. So in principle there is always a *JC* wage

increase large enough that it would guarantee that a tax would improve total welfare. An

empirically-based prediction of a *JC* wage increase would not by itself indicate that it was large

enough to cause the tax to be welfare-increasing. The predicted wage increase would have to be

larger than the critical wage increase derived from the model.

Another necessary condition is for a tax on *AW* firms to increase total welfare is that α_i must

vary across workers. To see why, suppose that α_i were equal to a constant ($\bar{\alpha}$) for all workers

(shirkers and non-shirkers).

Proposition 3: If $\alpha_i = \bar{\alpha}$ for all workers, then a tax or a ban on *AW* firms cannot be welfare-improving.

Proof: If all workers started out in *JC* firms, then obviously a tax or on *AW* firms would have no effect, so the interesting case is where at least some workers are start out in *AW* firms. Lemma 1 shows that all else equal shirkers get more utility from working in a *JC* firm than non-shirkers do. Since all shirkers are identical and all non-shirkers are identical, the only possible scenarios are: (i) all non-shirkers start out in *AW* firms and all shirkers are indifferent between *JC* and *AW* firms and so choose randomly; (ii) all shirkers start out in *JC* firms and all non-shirkers are indifferent and choose randomly; and (iii) all workers of both types start out in *AW* firms. Case (i) is not possible, as in that case the only workers in *JC* firms are shirkers, and so w_{JC} will be equal to zero, which violates the assumption that $\eta > e$. Case (ii) cannot be a stable equilibrium, as a single additional non-shirker joining a *JC* firm would increase w_{JC}, breaking the indifference and causing all the other non-shirkers to follow. So Case (iii) is the only relevant one, and the only relevant policy is a tax high enough to cause all workers to switch from *AW* to *JC* firms (i.e., a ban).[12]

Since *JC* firms are more attractive to shirkers than to otherwise equivalent non-shirkers, the requirement for the policy to be effective is that it must cause all non-shirkers to want to switch from *AW* to *JC* firms. When all workers are in *JC* firms, the *JC* wage will be at its highest possible level w_{JC}^{MAX}.

(12)
$$w_{JC}^{MAX} = \frac{\frac{\eta + \rho\eta}{2} N^{NS}}{N^{NS} + N^S}$$

---

[12] This is the scenario considered in Levine (1991).

22

Firms will only offer that wage if they believe that their workforce will have the same proportion of shirkers as in the general population. An AW ban guarantees that this will be the case. But an individual JC firm can also offer a wage w_{JC}^{MAX} and guarantee itself the population proportion of shirkers. The reason is that *all* workers prefer JC firms at that wage, and so an individual firm could guarantee itself the population proportion of shirkers simply by hiring at random from the applicant pool. Since the market generates the same outcome that a ban would, the ban cannot be welfare improving. ∎

Proposition 3 holds because the applicant pool for firms that pay a wage of w_{JC}^{MAX} contains the population proportion of shirkers. This will not be the case if there is some costly action that can be taken to increase the chances of getting a JC job. Shirkers will be more willing to bear that cost and so the applicant pool will consist disproportionately of shirkers. A "mobility" cost that shirkers are prepared to bear and non-shirkers are not is what drives the result in Levine (1991), in which a ban on AW firms can be welfare-improving even though in that model all workers are assumed to be identical apart from whether or not they are shirkers.

D. Distributional Effects of a Total Welfare-Increasing Tax on AW firms.

A tax on AW firms that increases total welfare will not affect all workers equally. This is the subject of the following two propositions.

Proposition 4: All else equal a tax on AW firms that increases total welfare makes workers with the lowest values of α_i worse off, workers with the highest values α_i better off, and has an intermediate and ambiguous effect on workers with intermediate values of α_i.

Proof: Workers with the lowest values of α_i are infra-marginal AW workers, who are directly made worse off by the tax. The Corollary to Proposition 2 shows that for a tax or a ban on AW firms to increase total welfare, it must cause w_{JC} to increase. Since the workers with the highest values of α_i are infra-marginal JC workers, any total welfare increasing tax must raise their wage and makes them better off. Workers with intermediate values of α_i switch from AW to JC firms as a result of the tax. These workers are made better off if the tax causes w_{JC} to increase by enough. But if they do benefit it will be by less than the infra-marginal JC workers, as they preferred to work in AW firms at the pre-tax wage. Similarly, if they are made worse off, it will be by less than the infra-marginal AW workers. ∎

Proposition 5: All else equal, a tax on AW firms that increases total welfare benefits shirkers more than non-shirkers.

Proof: Proposition 4 shows that a tax that increases total welfare always benefits infra-marginal JC workers, has intermediate and ambiguous effects on marginal switchers, and always harms infra-marginal AW workers. Lemma 1 shows that $\alpha^{NS} > \alpha^{S}$, which means that shirkers will be more concentrated among the groups that benefit more from the tax. ∎

V. Discussion:

In the above analysis, the proportion of shirkers in the population was assumed to be exogenous. But it is possible that the desire of a worker to shirk depends on the firm's reputation for how it treats employees and/or that worker's attitude towards the employer, which may in turn be affected by the worker's treatment at the hands of past employers. That is, there may be some workers who only want to shirk if they believe that their employer is not loyal to them.

If this is the case, then firms will have an incentive to treat their workers better and thereby generate good will if the number of workers who wish to shirk only at a non-loyal employer is sufficiently large. But there may be external effects that cause firms to under-invest in loyalty. For example, if workers are mobile, then a firm that invests in loyalty in one period may not be able to enjoy the benefits of it in a future period. Also, it may be the case that gestures of loyalty involve industry-wide economies of scale,[13] so it is only worthwhile if a sufficiently large number of other firms are doing it, which will be the case if such gestures are mandatory.

If these conditions hold, the argument for a tax (or a ban) becomes stronger: if more workers having the experience of working in JC firms reduces the number of shirkers in the economy, and if individual firms do not realize the full benefit of bringing this about, then the benefits of a tax are greater. Recall that a tax achieves reduced aggregate disutility from job insecurity at the cost of more aggregate shirking and job mismatch. To the extent that a tax also has a dynamic effect of reducing the desire to shirk, the case for it becomes stronger. In other words, forcing employers to act loyal may lead to a better equilibrium in which fewer workers are required to endure job insecurity *and* in which fewer workers shirk.

Even in cases where a tax on at-will firms improves welfare, it would be difficult to actually identify the optimal tax. A better alternative, if possible, would be to find technological or other means that make it easier to distinguish low productivity due to shirking from low productivity due to skill obsolescence. If shirking could be clearly identified in a provable way, then firms would be able to fire shirkers while still keeping their "just-cause" commitments to non-shirkers, which would be an unambiguous improvement.

The basic idea of this paper can be applied to other settings as well. For example, some firms in some poor countries lock workers in their factories in order to prevent theft. The tradeoff in that case (workers bearing the disutility of being locked in vs. the economic cost of theft) is similar to the tradeoff in this paper (workers bearing the disutility of job insecurity vs. the economic cost of shirking and job mismatch). As in this paper, it is possible to show that the market equilibrium is not necessarily optimal, and so a tax or a ban on firms that lock their factories could be welfare-improving.[14]

VI. Conclusions:

In this paper we emphasize the tradeoff between maximizing output and reducing workers' exposure to negative exogenous shocks to their productivity. A policy that shifts workers from at-will to just-cause jobs will generate some job security benefits, but will also lead to more shirking and to more misallocated workers. The paper models a scenario in which externalities

---

[13] An example may be promising that workers will be dealt with by trained Human Resource professionals, which is only possible if enough firms do it to support specialized HR training programs.

arising from individual job choice decisions cause adverse selection of shirkers into just-cause jobs, so that there can fewer such jobs than is socially optimal. This raises the possibility that a tax or a ban on at-will firms can be welfare-improving.

Even a tax or a ban that increases total welfare will not improve welfare for all agents in the economy. It will benefit those workers who value job security the most, harm those workers who value it the least, and have intermediate and ambiguous effect on those in the middle. It will also tend to benefit shirkers more than non-shirkers.

---

[14] A draft of an earlier version of this paper that focuses on locked factories is available from upon request.

References:

Baker, George, Gibbs, Michael, and Holmstrom, Bengt. "The Internal Economics of the Firm: Evidence from Personnel Data." *Quarterly Journal of Economics* 109 (1994): 881-919.

Bertola, Giuseppe. "A Pure Theory of Job Security and Labour Income Risk." *Review of Economic Studies* 71 (2004): 43-61.

Blanchard, Olivier J., and Tirole, Jean. "The Joint Design of Unemployment Insurance and Employment Protection: A First Pass." *Journal of the European Economic Association* 6 (2008): 45-77.

Bulow, Jeremy I., and Summers, Lawrence H. "A Theory of Dual Labor Markets with Application to Industrial Policy, Discrimination, and Keynesian Unemployment." *Journal of Labor Economics* 4 (1986): 376-414.

Blanchard, Olivier J., and Tirole, Jean. "Redesigning the Employment Protection System." *De Economist* 152 (2004): 1-20.

Campbell, C. M., III and Kamlani, K. S. "The Reasons for Wage Rigidity: Evidence from a Survey of Firms." *Quarterly Journal of Economics* 112 (1997): 759-789.

DiNardo, John, Fortin, Nicole, and Lemieux, Thomas "Labor Market Institutions and the Distribution of Wages, 1973-1992: A Semiparametric Approach." *Econometrica* 64 (1996): 1001-1044.

Frank, R. H. "Are Workers Paid their Marginal Product?" *American Economic Review* 74 (1984): 549-571.

Levine, David I. "Just-Cause Employment Policies in the Presence of Worker Adverse Selection." *Journal of Labor Economics* 9 (1991): 294-305.

Ljungqvist, Lars, and Thomas J. Sargent, "The European Unemployment Dilemma." *Journal of Political Economy* 106 (1998): 514-550

MacLeod, W. Bentley., and Voraprapa, Nakavachara. "Can Wrongful Discharge Law Enhance Employment?" *Economic Journal* 117 (2007): F218-F278.

Pissarides, Christopher A. "Employment Protection." *Labour Economics* 8 (2001): 131-59.

Appendix

<u>Proof of Lemma 2:</u>

For the uniform distribution, the middle segment of curve **A** is from $\{N_{JC}^{NS}, N_{JC}^{S}, w_{JC}\}$

$$\{0, \frac{2eN^S}{\alpha^{max}-\alpha^{min}}, \frac{\eta+\rho\eta+(1-\rho)\theta-\alpha^{max}}{2}\} \text{ to}$$

$$\{\frac{[(\alpha^{max}-\alpha^{min})-2e]N^{NS}}{\alpha^{max}-\alpha^{min}}, N^S, \frac{\eta+\rho\eta+(1-\rho)\theta-2e-\alpha^{min}}{2}\}, \text{ and the relationship between the two}$$

types of labor is $N_{JC}^{S} = \frac{2eN^S}{\alpha^{max}-\alpha^{min}} + \frac{N^S}{N^{NS}}N_{JC}^{NS}$. Substituting this into equation (5), we get:

$$(A1) \qquad w_{JC} = \frac{\left(\dfrac{\eta+\rho\eta}{2}\right)N_{JC}^{NS}}{N_{JC}^{NS}+\dfrac{2eN^S}{\alpha^{max}-\alpha^{min}}+\dfrac{N^S}{N^{NS}}N_{JC}^{NS}}$$

This allows us to take derivatives following along the middle line segment. The first and second derivatives are:

$$(A2) \qquad \frac{(\eta+\rho\eta)\dfrac{2eN^S}{\alpha^{max}-\alpha^{min}}}{2\left(\dfrac{2eN^S}{\alpha^{max}-\alpha^{min}}+\left(1+\dfrac{N^S}{N^{NS}}\right)N_{JC}^{NS}\right)^2}$$

$$(A3) \qquad \frac{-\left(1+\dfrac{N^S}{N^{NS}}\right)(\eta+\rho\eta)\dfrac{2eN^S}{\alpha^{max}-\alpha^{min}}}{\left(\dfrac{2eN^S}{\alpha^{max}-\alpha^{min}}+\left(1+\dfrac{N^S}{N^{NS}}\right)N_{JC}^{NS}\right)^3}$$

Since all parameters are positive and non-zero, it is apparent that the first derivative is positive and the second derivative is strictly negative. Thus as we move along the attainable choices of labor, equation (5) is increasing and strictly concave. And as we moved along the attainable choices of labor, the middle segment of curve **A** was increasing and linear. Thus it follows that equation (5) crosses the middle segment of curve **A** at zero to two points. ∎

<u>Proof of Lemma 3, Uniform Distribution:</u>

Let α_i be distributed U[a,b] for both shirkers and non-shirkers, and let $b > \alpha^{NS} > \alpha^{S} > a$. At the unregulated equilibrium, the proportion of non-shirkers among the workers in JC firms is:

28

$$(A4) \qquad \frac{N^{NS} \int_{\alpha^{NS}}^{b} \frac{1}{b-a} d\alpha}{N^{NS} \int_{\alpha^{NS}}^{b} \frac{1}{b-a} d\alpha + N^{S} \int_{\alpha^{S}}^{b} \frac{1}{b-a} d\alpha} = \frac{N^{NS}(b-\alpha^{NS})}{b(N^{NS}+N^{S}) - N^{NS}\alpha^{NS} - N^{S}\alpha^{S}}$$

As guaranteed by Lemma 1, this proportion is less than the population proportion of non-shirkers. The tax causes both thresholds to decrease by Δ. The mass of non-shirkers who switch from AW to JC firms as a result is:

$$(A5) \qquad N^{NS} \int_{\alpha^{NS}-\Delta}^{b} \frac{1}{b-a} d\alpha - N^{NS} \int_{\alpha^{NS}}^{b} \frac{1}{b-a} d\alpha = \frac{\Delta N^{NS}}{b-a}$$

The mass of shirkers who switch from AW to JC firms is:

$$(A6) \qquad N^{S} \int_{\alpha^{S}-\Delta}^{b} \frac{1}{b-a} d\alpha - N^{S} \int_{\alpha^{S}}^{b} \frac{1}{b-a} d\alpha = \frac{\Delta N^{S}}{b-a}$$

The proportion of non-shirkers among switchers is:

$$(A7) \qquad \frac{N^{NS}}{N^{NS}+N^{S}}$$

The uniform distribution guarantees that the proportion of non-shirkers among the marginal switchers will be equal to the population proportion of non-shirkers. It is straightforward to show that ($A7$) must be greater than ($A4$). ∎

Proof of Lemma 3, U-Quadratic Distribution:
For a tax to make the JC wage decrease, the proportion of non-shirkers among marginal switchers must be smaller than the proportion among infra-marginal JC workers. Let α_i be distributed U-quadratic on $[a,b]$ for both shirkers and non-shirkers,[15] and let $b > \alpha^{NS} > \alpha^{S} > a$. Choose parameter values such that $\alpha^{NS} = (a+b)/2$. At the unregulated equilibrium, the proportion of non-shirkers among the workers in JC firms is:

$$(A8) \qquad \frac{N^{NS} \int_{\frac{a+b}{2}}^{b} x(\alpha-y)^2 d\alpha}{N^{NS} \int_{\frac{a+b}{2}}^{b} x(\alpha-y)^2 d\alpha + N^{S} \int_{\frac{a+b}{2}-2e}^{b} x(\alpha-y)^2 d\alpha} = \frac{N^{NS}}{N^{NS} + \frac{N^{S}\left((b-a)^3 + 64e^3\right)}{(b-a)^3}}$$

---

[15] The pdf of the U-quadratic distribution is $x(\alpha-y)^2$, where $x = 12/(b-a)^3$ and $y = (a+b)/2$.

As guaranteed by Lemma 1, this proportion is less than the population proportion of non-shirkers. The tax causes both thresholds to decrease by Δ. The mass of non-shirkers who switch from AW to JC firms as a result is:

$$(A9) \qquad N^{NS} \int_{\frac{a+b}{2}-\Delta}^{b} x(\alpha-y)^2 \, d\alpha - N^{NS} \int_{\frac{a+b}{2}}^{b} x(\alpha-y)^2 \, d\alpha = \frac{4N^{NS}\Delta^3}{(b-a)^3}$$

The mass of shirkers who switch from AW to JC firms is:

$$(A10) \qquad N^{S} \int_{\frac{a+b}{2}-2e-\Delta}^{b} x(\alpha-y)^2 \, d\alpha - N^{S} \int_{\frac{a+b}{2}-2e}^{b} x(\alpha-y)^2 \, d\alpha = \frac{4N^{S}\Delta\left(12e^2+6e\Delta+\Delta^2\right)}{(b-a)^3}$$

The proportion of non-shirkers among switchers is:

$$(A11) \qquad \frac{N^{NS}\Delta^2}{(N^{NS}+N^{S})\Delta^2 + N^{S}(12e^2+6e\Delta)}$$

If $b = 1$, $a = 0$, $e = 1/8$, $\Delta = \frac{1}{4}$, $N^{NS} = 95$, and $N^{S} = 5$, then $(A11)$ is smaller than $(A8)$, and so the tax makes the JC wage decrease. ∎

30

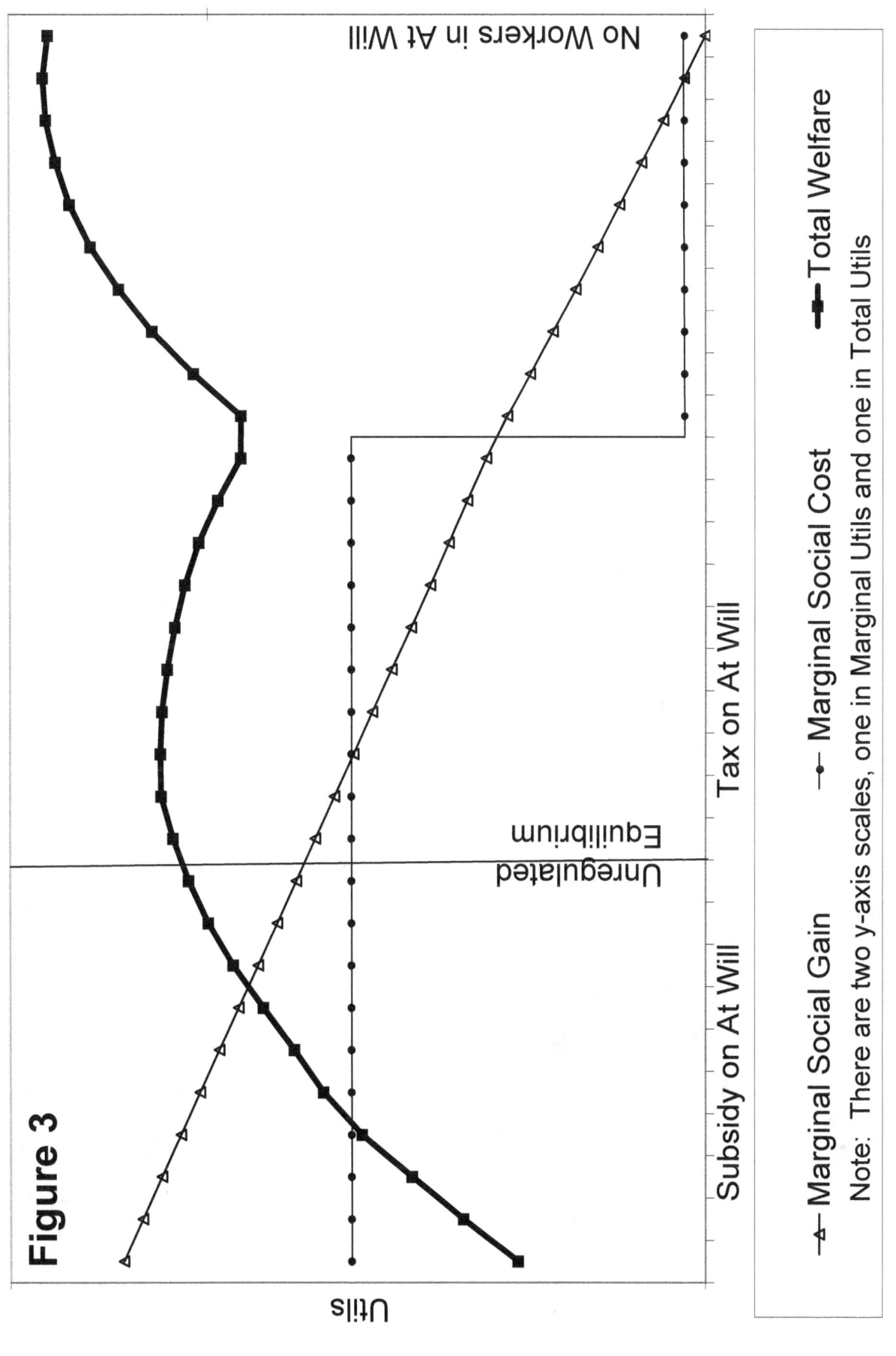

Figure 3

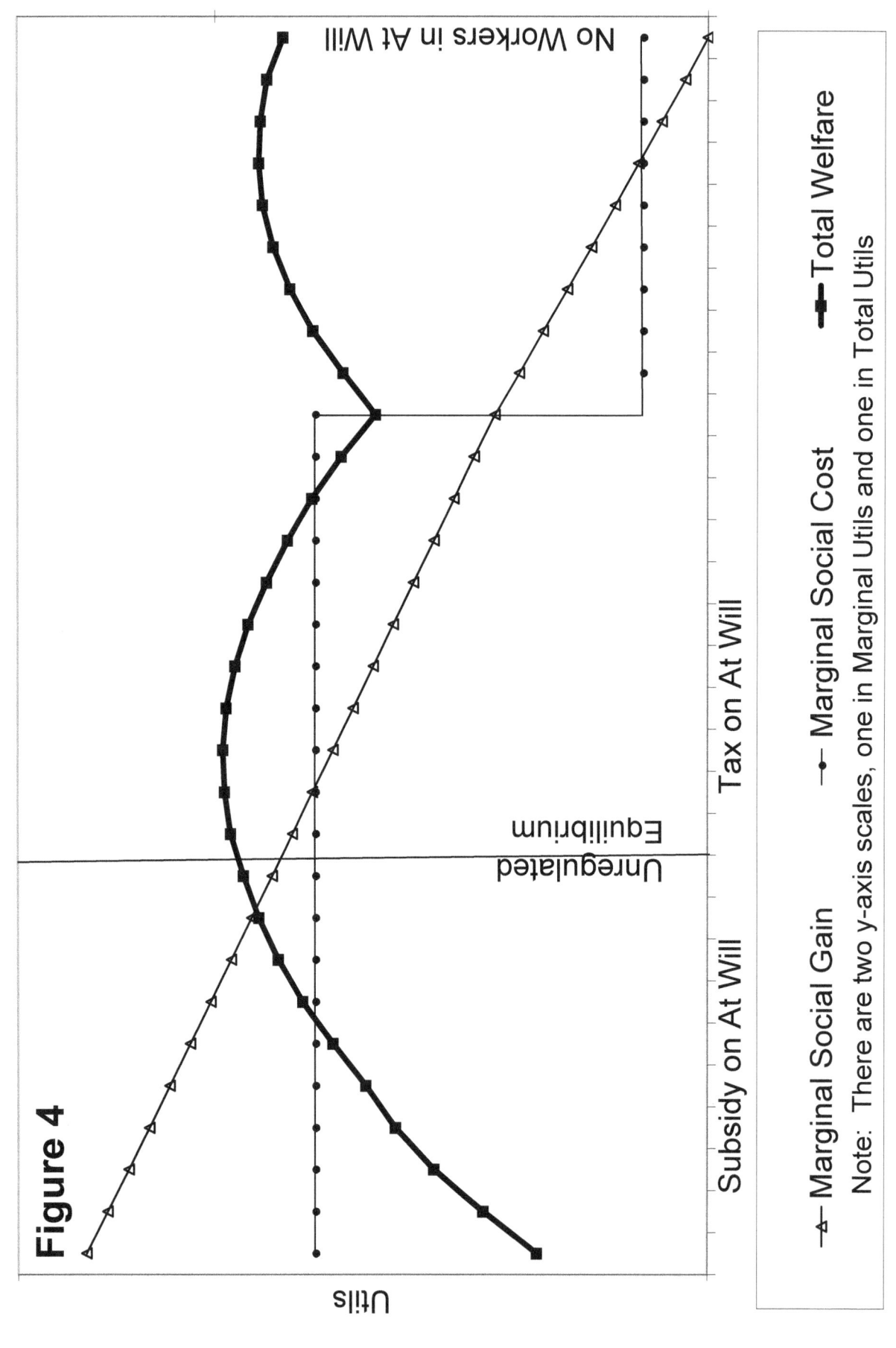

Figure 4

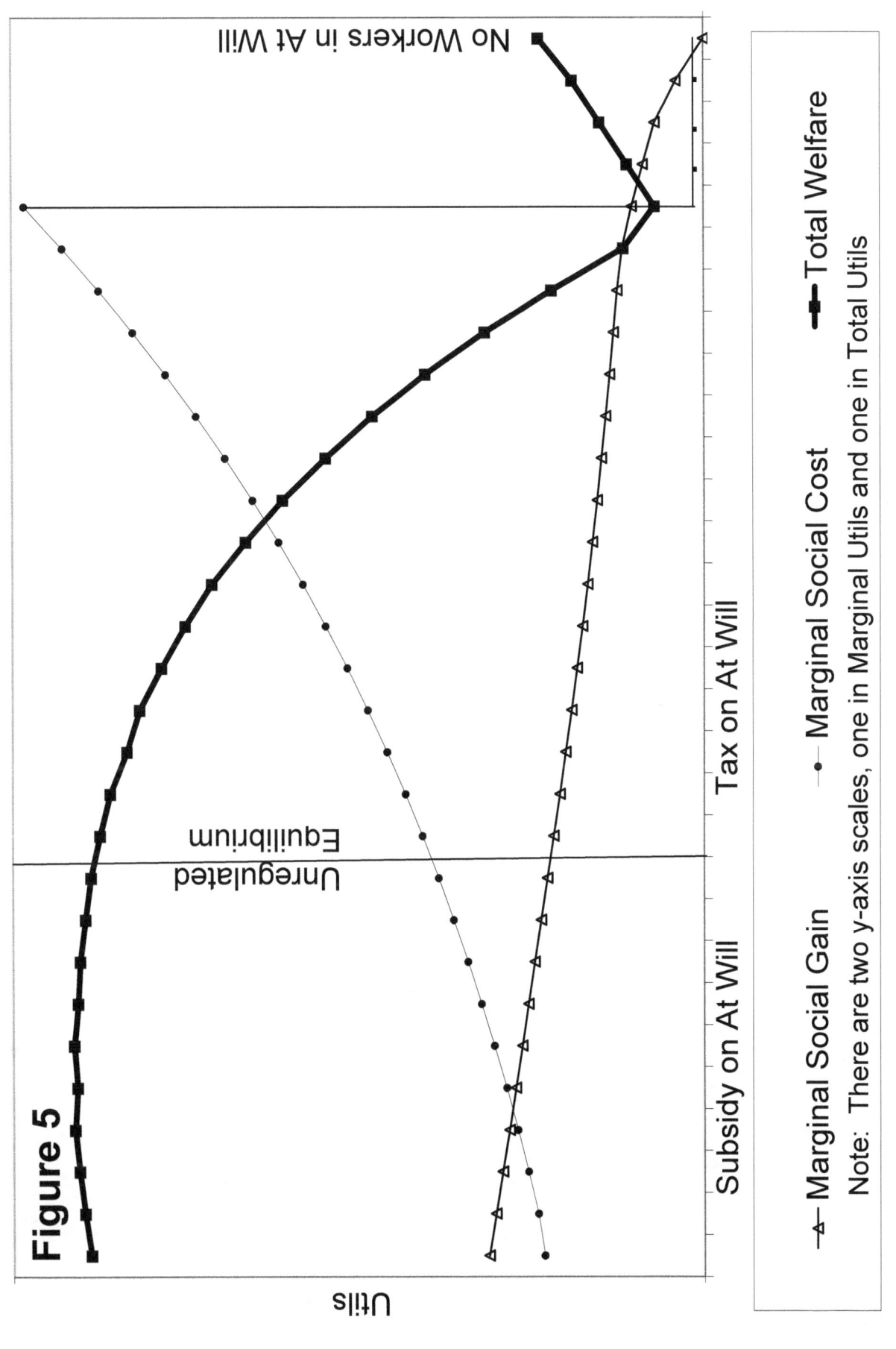

Figure 5

www.ingramcontent.com/pod-product-compliance
Lightning Source LLC
Chambersburg PA
CBHW081245170526
45165CB00009B/3196